GOOD ✦ OLD ✦ DAYS

Live It Again™
1945

Dear Friends,

If there was a year in which we sought to return to the status quo, it was 1945. The year began with its own type of status quo when U.S. President Franklin D. Roosevelt was sworn in for his unprecedented fourth term in office. The beloved President Roosevelt initially took the presidential reins in 1932, the darkest days of the Great Depression.

But just as the first rays of hope were beginning to beam through the storm of the European and Pacific Ocean Theatres of World War II, President Roosevelt suffered a massive stroke on April 12 and died within hours.

FDR never got to see the end of the war nor our return to the status quo. The collapse of Berlin and V-E Day on May 8 provided relief on that front, but the war raged on in the South Pacific. It took the horror of two great bombs—Little Boy and Fat Man—on Hiroshima and Nagasaki on Aug. 6 and 9 to bring Japan to its knees.

FDR never got to see our return to the status quo.

No photograph encapsulated the sheer joy of the announcement of the war's end than that of famed *Life* magazine photographer Alfred Eisenstaedt of a jubilant sailor kissing a nurse in New York City's Times Square on Aug. 14 (see page 85). Into the vacuum of a world finally at peace came an almost frenzied desire to return to a sense of normalcy.

This special yearbook will take you through those divergent halves—war and peace, chaos and calm—of 1945. In these pages, you will take a captivating visual tour of this important year in American history.

In addition to the big wartime events, you'll enjoy sweeter reminders of the way we were. You'll meet sports stars, including the members of the All-American Girls Baseball League—the women who worked hard to keep America's pastime going during the war. We'll show you the fashion-setting trends, the movie stars turning heads and the recording artists making us swoon.

It was all part of how we returned to the status quo in that pivotal year of 1945.

Contents

REPRINTED WITH PERMISSION OF MICHELIN NORTH AMERICA

1945 GABY SUNTAN LOTION

REPRINTED WITH PERMISSION FROM FORD MOTOR CO

80-G-377094, NATIONAL ARCHIVES

1945 HART SCHAFFNER & MARX

Neighborhood clothing stores were neatly designed to showcase the latest in outerwear, complete with designs of properly meshed color schemes.

FAMOUS BIRTHDAYS
Rod Stewart, January 10 British rock singer
Tom Selleck, January 29 actor

Going to the grocery store was quite the shopping affair, from the popcorn vendor on the outside to the fresh produce displays and penny-candy counters on the inside.

MEATS FOODS GROCERIES

In the Neighborhood

Where we shopped

The expression "heading downtown" in 1945 meant a shopping trip to one of the local department stores, usually located in the center of town or neighborhood. Clothing, hardware and grocery stores were all places to meet and catch up on the latest news from neighbors. Owners would stock their inventory according to the known needs of their customers.

Often, popcorn machines and hot dog vendors dotted street corners to add to the charm of shopping days for the entire family. Children shook their banks for a few coins to spend in the toy sections of variety stores. On occasion, a sack of chocolate-covered candies topped off the special outing.

The general store usually had a gathering place to have a cup of coffee, perhaps smoke a pipe and tell tales of years gone by.

The coming of asphalt tile ware provided cleaner and safer floors for those visiting more formal businesses such as drugstores and offices.

World War II created numerous "boomtowns" associated with manufacturing of various products for use at battle sites. These grocery clerks worked in Oak Ridge, Tenn., site of several uranium-235 extraction facilities.

In the Neighborhood

At your service

The personal touch of service created business bonding and friendships that strengthened the sense of community in neighborhoods. Service station attendants cleaned windshields, checked fluids and often provided treats for children. Mailmen would deliver packages with a friendly greeting and sometimes there would be a brief visit before delivery continued.

At corner markets, free samples of candy and other products would often be given to customers as an added touch of kindness from owners. People took the time to help a neighbor in need along the way and everyone watched out for the elderly and those with special situations in their neighborhood. Those being served would return acts of kindness during special holidays with homemade goodies or other small gifts.

Many businesses provided stamps with purchases that could lead to redemption for household products at a certain point of collection.

The Metro Daily News
FINAL EDITION

THE WEATHER
City and State—Rain, Snow, Colder

VOLUME 11—No. 191

JANUARY 20, 1945

FRANKLIN D. ROOSEVELT SWORN-IN FOR AN UNPRECEDENTED FOURTH TERM AS PRESIDENT OF THE UNITED STATES

Careful and conscientious service was provided with courtesy and concern.

Service station attendants took time to add fluids and make necessary provisions to assist with car care.

Mail was often delivered with a personal greeting and warm smile along with the latest tidbits of information from around the neighborhood.

Those making home improvements did not rush through the jobs and added personalized practical advice their services. Their work was reasonable and efficient because they were usually serving friends in the neighborhood.

A warm smile and quick visit often accompanied delivery of products to the front door.

Customers would special order baked items that were delivered through the corner market or directly to the home.

Coal was shoveled into the customer's coal bin by the delivery men. The product would be deposited through a basement window into a designated are not far from the furnace.

In the Neighborhood

Delivering the goods

The personal touch of business to residents was especially evident in the willingness to deliver products to the doorstep. Most homes placed milk boxes on the front porch where the milkman would deliver white and chocolate milk, and dairy products each morning. Delivering dairy products each morning throughout the neighborhood was a full-time job.

Children often looked forward to the bread truck that brought loaves of bread, rolls and other goodies to the front door. The familiar jingling of bells could often be heard when the ice cream truck drove through residential streets on hot summer afternoons selling popsicles and ice cream bars for a few cents.

Other home deliveries included coal and groceries, especially to those who had difficulty making it to the grocery store.

Moving day often involved an entire lineup of various sized trucks to assist with the project.

FAMOUS BIRTHDAYS
Bob Griese, February 3 football player
Barry Bostwick, February 24 actor

Those delivering products to neighborhood groceries always had time for a quick chat with children.

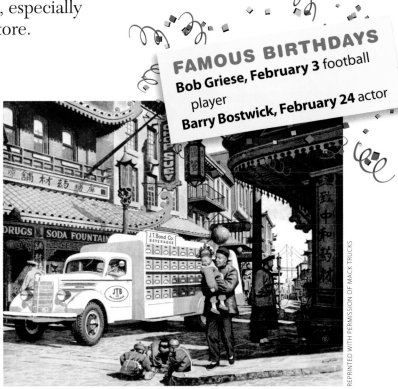

Delivery of soft drinks took place in open trucks, often enticing children to ask their parents for a bottle of soda like the ones they had seen on the truck.

Artist Tribute

Mead Shaeffer

A friend of Norman Rockwell, Mead Schaeffer was a war correspondent for *The Saturday Evening Post* and illustrated more than 15 military-themed covers. He was considered the most authentic storyteller of his time, due to his attention to detail. He was rarely satisfied with just imagining the soldier's life, but instead hitched rides with the servicemen for eye-witness views of the action.

Mead was the son of a preacher and grew up in Springfield, Mass. Here, through his father's vocation, he experienced a wide range of life milestones that are the common theme of a simple life, providing later creative inspiration. Mead quickly caught the attention of great illustration teachers and soon began work with smaller traditional magazines. After marrying, he moved to Vermont, where he converted an old barn into a studio. It was here he became best friends with Norman Rockwell. The two artists often found themselves as subjects of the other's artwork.

After the war years, Mead continued his longstanding relationship with Rockwell and *The Post*. In the span of his career, he created over 5,000 illustrations of which 46 were *Post* covers. A number of his *Post* covers are shown at right.

This *Post* cover by Schaeffer from April 1945 is an apt representation of the time period and the focus of the year, World War II.

© 1945 SEPS

What Made Us Laugh

At first glance one might question this Norman Rockwell painting that appeared on the March 31, 1945, *Post* cover. Rockwell decided to have some fun and painted 51 mistakes in honor of April Fool's Day. The model for this painting was Rockwell's friend and neighbor, artist John Atherton whose paintings were featured on many *Post* covers. Try finding all of the 51 mistakes without looking at the answers given below.

Answers to the April-Fool cover

1. Apples on maple tree.
2. Different-color apples.
3. Baseball among apples.
4. Pine boughs.
5. Pine cone should point down under bough.
6. Horse-chestnut leaves.
7. Grapes.
8. April 1st comes on Sunday, not Monday.
9. Penguins don't fly.
10. Halo.
11. Nest on phone.
12. Different-color eggs.
13. Phone wire on wrong end of receiver.
14. Different or wrong color butterflies.
15. Books on tree.
16. Castle in landscape.
17. Lighthouse and ship.
18. Earmuffs.
19. Fur collar on velvet jacket.
20. Two different designs on shirt.
21. Shirt buttoned wrong way.
22. Life jacket.
23. Three hands.
24. Cigarette and pipe used at same time.
25. Collar and necktie on bird.
26. Fly-casting reel on bait-casting rod.
27. Cloth patches on waders.
28. Rod upside down.
29. Alligators as roots.
30. Cobra in mandolin.
31. Ribbon on mandolin.
32. Post heading on wrong side of magazine.
33. Snow scene.
34. Horizons different on two scenes.
35. Horns on mouse's head.
36. Animal head on turtle.
37. You're wrong; there are blue lobsters although they are extremely unusual freaks of nature. I once saw one!
38. Tomato picture on plum can.
39. House slippers on skis.
40. Shells.
41. Dutchman's-breeches.
42. Lady's-slipper.
43. Buttercup.
44. Thimbleweed.
45. Bachelor-buttons.
46. Poison ivy.
47. Signature upside down.
48. Skis without back.
49. Lead sinkers on line should be below floater.
50. Floater upside down.
51. Red should be at top of floater in right position.

–Norman Rockwell

"Does mother go around making nasty remarks about that silly little cap you wear?"

"Just think of its convenience! You're out in the middle of the lake—all by yourself—suddenly your wife decides she wants to talk to you—!"

USE IT UP – WEAR IT OUT – MAKE IT DO!

OUR LABOR AND OUR GOODS ARE FIGHTING

Every American citizen was part of the war effort through conservative efforts at home from patching worn-out clothes to taking a garment and remaking it into a different style.

During World War II, gas was rationed and in short supply. Companies often advertised the energy saving qualities of their products.

Even children supported our troops by collecting old newspapers from the neighborhood. Paper salvage was a necessity. The military used large quantities for intelligence as well as for wrapping supplies and ammunition.

On the Home Front

We all supported our troops

There was a war to be won and those on the home front were determined to do their part. Gas rationing was in full force during 1945. Every drop was conserved even when Americans didn't feel like "squeezing the gas hose" any more. There was a serious shortage of all types of paper, including photographic material, with only small amounts left for civilian use. This was a military necessity, as photographs were the "eyes" of intelligence. Civilians even made do by patching worn clothing instead of buying new. Many women made quilts from scraps for gifts to servicemen or to raise money for good causes.

HELP BRING THEM BACK TO YOU!

Find time for war work

Raise and share food

Walk and carry packages

Conserve everything you have

Save 10% in War Bonds

THIS IS A V HOME

A VICTORY HOME!

Victory quilts were made as gifts for servicemen or as raffle items to raise money for good causes, such as the Red Cross. Quilts shown above are from a very informative book titled *World War II Quilts* by Sue Reich.

Homes of servicemen were often obvious from the flags and stars on display. Posters were also placed in windows declaring , "This is a V home."

On the Home Front

Buying war bonds

In 1945, the United States Treasury Dept. developed many ways of promoting and selling war bonds. One way was through releasing a short movie in theaters entitled *My Japan*. The production gave the narration from the Japanese perspective and described Japan in positive terms while mocking Americans. The movie was designed to raise the emotion of Americans in ways that motivated them to purchase bonds. Many businesses including Sears encouraged the purchase of war bonds as Christmas and birthday gifts.

Bonds were sold for as little as $18.75 and matured to $25 in 10 years. Large denominations of between $50 and $1,000 were also made available. The War Finance Committee was placed in charge of supervising the sale of all bonds. Over the course of the war, 85 million Americans purchased bonds totaling approximately $185.7 billion.

BACK 'EM UP

BUY EXTRA BONDS

Mothers taught children that purchasing bonds was a way of speeding up the time so that their fathers could come home sooner. It was also looked upon as a way of saving for postwar prosperity.

They're fighting harder than ever

are you buying MORE WAR BONDS THAN EVER?

Posters encouraged Americans to conti purchasing war bonds. This participatio was a way in which citizens showed sol they were also making sacrifices.

1945 ADEL PRECISION PRODUCTS CORP.

LIBERTY FOR ALL

KEEP 'EM FLYING

Uncle Sam says:
"Take care of your car, brother
—no telling when
you'll be sure of
a new one!"

KEEP ON BUYING WAR BONDS, TOO!

Uncle Sam was often featured on a poster or advertisement promoting the purchase of war bonds.

Our Boys Need Your Help!

The Metro Daily News

FINAL EDITION

FEBRUARY 19, 1945

BATTLE OF IWO JIMA STARTS

Approximately 30,000 United States Marines land on Iwo Jima. This battle officially ends on March 26, 1945.

Keeping morale of the troops high was important during World War II. Watching movies reminded soldiers of home.

United States soldiers in a military hospital lifted their spirits as they join in song around a piano.

FAMOUS BIRTHDAYS
Dirk Benedict, March 1 actor
Pat Riley, March 20 basketball coach

Bing Crosby, Hollywood star, sings to Allied troops at London, England. The soldiers felt these shows did more for them than a double dose of vitamins.

Entertaining Our Troops

The United Service Organization (USO) was a private, nonprofit organization that provided morale and recreational services to the United States military. During World War II, it became the GI's "home away from home." Through live shows, called Camp Shows, the entertainment industry helped boost morale. Hollywood was eager to show its patriotism, and many big names entertained both at home and overseas, often placing their own lives in danger by traveling or performing under hazardous conditions. During the war more than 400,000 performances were presented, including such entertainers as Bing Crosby, Judy Garland, Bette Davis, Frank Sinatra, Lauren Bacall, Danny Kaye, Marlene Dietrich, Mickey Rooney, Lucille Ball and, most famously, Bob Hope. Bob Hope traveled and entertained the troops tirelessly, and his humor provided a welcomed respite for United States forces.

Danny Kaye, well-known stage and screen star, has fun while entertaining 4,000 troops at Sasebo, Japan. The sign across the front of the stage says, "Officers keep out! Enlisted men's country."

Mickey Rooney, actor and entertainer, brings [hum]or to the troops in Germany as he imitates [th]e Hollywood actors.

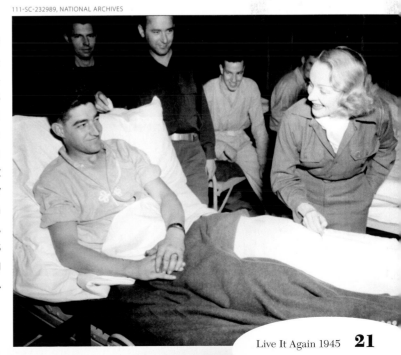

Marlene Dietrich, actress, autographs the cast on the leg of an American soldier at a military hospital in Belgium, where she is entertaining the GIs.

Women in the Military

Women's lives changed in many ways during World War II. As with most wars, women found their roles, opportunities and responsibilities expanded. Women served in many positions in direct support of the World War II military efforts. Military women were excluded from combat positions, but that didn't keep some from being in harm's way, such as nurses in or near combat zones or on ships. About 74,000 women served as nurses in the war effort. Women also served in other military branches, often in traditional "women's work" such as secretarial duties or cleaning. Others took traditional men's jobs in non-combat military work to free more men for combat. More than 1,000 women served as pilots associated with the armed forces, but were considered civil service workers and weren't recognized for their military service for many more years.

The military-issued war helmets were used for everything from a footbath basin to a seat in the movies.

Among an Army nurse's sacrifices were the manly living quarters.

Women freed more men for combat duty by demonstrating their ability to work at what were considered traditionally men's jobs.

Women's Army Auxiliary Corps (WAAC) officers go shopping soon after their arrival at an army base. Members of the WAAC were the first women other than nurses to serve in the ranks of the Army.

o one will ever know how any vital war errands were n by women, likely saving untless lives.

Many women became nurses during the war and were commissioned in the United States Army, leaving home for duty.

Medics from the Army's 10th Mountain Division bring down a casualty from a mountain-top skirmish in Italy. Soldiers from this division experienced some of the worst terrain and bitterest weather of the war.

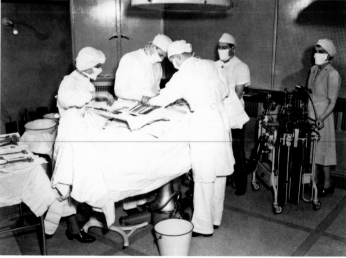

This military hospital in England represents many treatment centers where wounded were sent for surgery and recovery.

Caring for Our Wounded

Caring for the wounded during World War II was one of the most difficult and dangerous responsibilities. It was the medic's job to get the wounded away from the front lines. Often this involved a medic climbing from the protection of his own foxhole during the heat of battle to carry his comrade to safety.

There was an 85 percent chance of recovery for wounded soldiers during World War II if a medic could get to him within the first hour. Drugs such as sulfa and penicillin made recovery more possible. Those caring for the wounded also had access to more advanced surgical techniques. The overall speed with which wounded were treated greatly improved the rate of recovery.

Mountain engineers constructed a tramway to evacuate the wounded from a 1,600-foot mountain battleground. The descent required four minutes by tram and about four laborious hours by foot.

Soldiers who were wounded in Europe's battlefields are being transported to various hospitals in the United States by train. Providing sleeping cars for the recovering soldier was Pullman's way of supporting our troops.

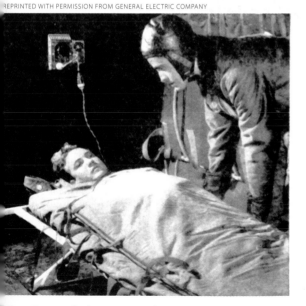

The General Electric Co. supplied the military with electrically heated "casualty blankets" that automatically maintained protective warmth in temperatures as low as 60 degrees below zero.

The Roosevelt family gathered for this family portrait on Inauguration Day, Jan. 20, 1945.

President Roosevelt and Gen. Dwight Eisenhower review troops on a Sicilian airfield. Gen. George Patton is pictured in the background.

1945 Presidents

On Jan. 20, 1945, Franklin D. Roosevelt was sworn into office beginning his fourth term as president of the United States. This fourth term ended abruptly on April 12 with his sudden death at Warm Springs, Ga. After a White House funeral on April 14, his body was transported back to Hyde Park, N.Y., where he was buried on April 15 in the rose garden of the Springwood Estate. During Roosevelt's 12 years in office, he led the country through some of its greatest crisis, working hard to ensure the close-at-hand World War II victories.

When Vice President Harry S. Truman became president on April 12, he was thrown into a whole arena of wartime problems to solve. Over the next few months he made some of the most crucial decisions in presidential history, including those which led to the dropping of the bombs on Hiroshima and Nagasaki to bring about a Japanese surrender.

The funeral procession of President Roosevelt prepares to make its journey to Hyde Park, N.Y.

President Harry S. Truman takes the oath of office on the evening of April 12, 1945, following the death of President Franklin D. Roosevelt. His wife Bess and daughter Margaret stand at his side in this solemn hour.

President Truman meets with several Cabinet members at the White House. From left to right: Secretary of State James F. Byrnes, President Truman, Secretary of the Treasury Fred M. Vinson and Attorney General Tom Clark.

President Truman and British Prime Minister Winston Churchill have an informed chat at Mr. Churchill's residence in the Berlin area while attending the Potsdam Conference in July 1945.

A beauty fad of the time, warm mud was applied to the skin to retain a fresh, young complexion.

© 1945 SEPS

Movie star Ingrid Bergman's appearance was copied by many. The look was glamorous, but in a very subdued, sophisticated way. Having a Pepsodent smile with the perfect shade of red lipstick only added to one's beauty.

The Metro Daily News

FINAL EDITION

MARCH 15, 1945

THE 17TH ACADEMY AWARDS ARE BROADCAST IN ITS ENTIRETY ON RADIO FOR THE FIRST TIME

They are broadcast on ABC and the Armed Forces Radio.

1945 PEPSODENT TOOTHPASTE

1945 Style

Prep time for women

With World War II drawing to a close, women wanted to look their best to greet soldiers returning home. More women went to beauty shops for popular, but uncomfortable permanent waves. Hair was wound on heavy metal rods connected by wires to electricity for heat. The procedure lasted three hours or more and sometimes resulted in headaches or burned scalps along with curls. Some women indulged in warm mud baths, thought to retain youthfulness and improve complexions. Women's underwear had evolved in favor of two-piece arrangements including a girdle, which replaced the corset.

1945 KOHLER OF KOHLER

From her lovely pageboy hairdo to her pretty frilly dress, decorated with a demure flower at the ruffled neckline, this young lady is the picture of 1940s innocence and beauty.

Permanent-wave machines looked very strange, with separate electrical wires leading to each chemical-wrapped curl. The question here is who was more afraid—the mouse or the lady getting the perm?

"I don't want to wear it—I just want to scare myself into staying on my diet."

1945 Style

Women looking their best

Wartime austerity led to restrictions on the number of new clothes that women bought and the amount of fabric clothing manufacturers could use. Women still managed to look good through previously overlooked American designers while European fashion was not available. Most women wore skirts at or near knee-length, with simply-cut blouses, sweaters and square-shouldered jackets. Popular magazines and pattern companies advised women on how to remake men's suits into smart outfits since the men were in uniform and the cloth would otherwise be unused. The nylon stocking, though popular, was taken off the market briefly as all supplies were needed for military uses, such as parachutes. Hair was worn high over the forehead in a puff or rolls, called the pompadour.

Gloves were enormously important in 1945, with evening gowns accompanied by elbow-length versions.

In 1945 cloth was rationed and in short supply. Essential clothing, such as coats, were designed with simplicity and practicality in mind.

omen wore their
air at shoulder
ngth and Eisenhower
ckets became popular, the design
fluenced by the military.

Hats were worn for most
occasions and were decorated
with bits of netting, feathers,
ribbons or brooches.

Suntans were
fashionable along
with two-piece
swimsuits with
halter tops that
bared the midriff.

Gaby
GREASELESS
SUNTAN LOTION

Gaby
GREASELESS
SUNTAN LOTION

1945 Style

Men sprucing up and looking fine

In 1945, men wore suits for special occasions made from war-rationed materials. The colors of clothes remained somber, which signified the darkness of this time in history. Suit coats had heavily padded chests and enormous shoulders. The trousers were loose and wide flowing. Shirts sold for about $2 and ties for $1. Neckties were wide, and bold geometric designs were popular. An illicit item during the war was called the "zoot suit", an item that was usually worn in night clubs. It consisted of an oversized jacket, wide lapels, broad shoulders and pants narrowed towards the ankles. Men sometimes wore V-necked sweaters over a shirt for a more casual look. The usual hat of this period was the fedora, often worn tipped down over one eye at a rakish angle.

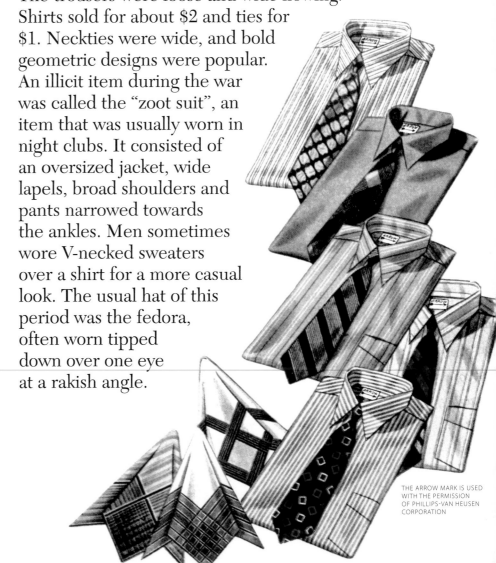

THE ARROW MARK IS USED WITH THE PERMISSION OF PHILLIPS-VAN HEUSEN CORPORATION

1945 MCGREGOR FASHION GROUP

Sweaters provided warmth during cool days.

© 1945 SEPS

"The hat just sets it off right. Just like I told the boys, 'Nothing's too good for my old supply sergeant!' "

Gabardine fabric was popular for suits that sold for $37.50 and up.

Hats for men had swank, easy lines and could be bought for around $10.

Shoes ranged in price from $5 to $10 a pair, with two-toned variations of the classic wingtip adding pizzaz.

FAMOUS BIRTHDAYS
Linda Hunt, April 2 actress
Tony Dow, April 13 actor,
(Leave It to Beaver)

Hattitudes

Hats were huge fashion accessories in 1945. The fashion-forward woman wore a hat for most occasions. This was the fashion of choice, but there was also a practical side. Women did not wash their hair frequently, and hats were the perfect cover-up for bad hair days. Millinery shops abounded and for the wealthy who could afford to pay top dollar, hats could be special ordered to match outfits. Hats were almost always worn perched on top of the head, tipped to the side and trimmed elaborately. World War II rationing limited fashion choices, but some items such as hats and embellishments could be purchased freely without coupons. Decorating hats became an artistic outlet for the creative woman. She could add a wide variety of trims, flowers, feathers, ribbons and veils to emphasize her own personal sense of style.

REPRINTED WITH PERMISSION FROM GENERAL ELECTRIC COMPANY

ED WITH PERMISSION FROM RUSSELL STOVER CANDIES

Shopping trips for women were seldom complete without a visit to the department store to pour over the latest styles in hats and trimmings.

REPRINTED WITH PERMISSION OF PHILIPS COMPANY ARCHIVES

TOM HENDERSON

"That's the most inexpensive hat we've had in stock for a long time!"

City Life

The city abounded with possibilities for entertainment. An evening away from home could be kept simple with a visit to one of the many movie theaters available. Or, for those with a bit more money to spend, the nightclub experience involved dinner, drinks, dancing and entertainment. Whether it was music or comedy, these big-city establishments were guaranteed to have the best performers around. Most large hotels had restaurants and ballrooms, often with their own orchestras and radio shows.

You could never go hungry in the city, where there were restaurants of all sizes and types. Italian and Chinese restaurants served up Americanized versions of their native cuisines. People soon fell in love with dishes like chop suey, pizza and spaghetti with meatballs.

Movies were affordable for most, and many pleasant evenings were spent in movie theaters. Troubles were swept away by the romances and adventures shown on the big screen.

"Something tells me we're going to find this place crowded too."

Romantic encounters often began at nightclubs with a glance across a crowded room.

"Don't worry, dear. I brought some sandwiches."

Nothing was more glamorous than visiting the most elegant hotel in town, riding the elevator to the rooftop ballroom and dancing the night away.

People had lunch with their friends, or met at a restaurant for pie, coffee and conversation.

PHOTOGRAPHY BY ARTHUR GRIFFIN, REPRINTED WITH PERMISSION OF GRIFFIN MUSEUM OF PHOTOGRAPHY

A view from Brewer Fountain looking toward the State House on Beacon Hill.

The statue commemorating Paul Revere's famous ride is shown in the foreground, with Old North Church in the background.

Old and new combined to give Boston the charm and spirit that made her great. The Park Street Church is shown in the foreground of this photo.

Boston in 1945

Boston was a complex, fascinating and distinctive city. Full of contrasts, people were rich while government was poor. The mayor of 1945 was Maurice Tobin until he was elected governor of Massachusetts; then John Kerrigan became acting mayor. The factories of the city were retooled for the war effort, making Boston a major arms manufacturer. Prosperity continued with the development of service industries, such as banking and finance. Boston was the third most important money market in the nation in 1945.

In 1945, Boston was a bustling city of over 700,000. A main source of entertainment was the city's professional baseball team, the Red Sox, located at Fenway Park. Many pleasant memories were made at the ballpark. On any given night, famous pitchers could be seen hurling the ball for a potential home run by a living legend.

Boston's fish business is older than the town itself and survived through ebbs and flows of the factories.

Some of Boston's oldest homes on Beacon Street, where many of the city's elite resided in 1945, featured bay windows.

Left: The Public Garden which was set aside over 300 years ago as a common pasture. Right: The Customs House Tower and Boston's tallest building in 1945 in the background.

Everyday Life

The family dog

The family dog was a great source of companionship and comfort during the difficult war times of 1945. In homes where fathers and siblings were off to battle, a hug for Fido or a big laugh at Rover would serve as a healing moment for a family lonesome for loved ones.

Moments of tossing a ball or catching the dog getting into a fresh batch of cookies were good distractions from troublesome realities. A good walk through the forest with the mutt, learning life lessons through the birth of pups or having a good chat on a lonely hillside were all special moments that taught secrets of friendship for years to come.

Pets would often greet their owners with such gifts as a slipper, towel or sock. Nothing was more meaningful than the unconditional loyalty of the family dog.

Even Butch the beloved *Post* cover dog has to sometimes watch his weight. No more sweet treats for him.

The family pet was always up for a bike ride or quality time going somewhere with his master.

Dogs fostered a spirit of loyalty and protection and watched over and cared for the members of their family.

ping clothespins to the ears is one way
eep Butch's ears out of his milk and keep
well-groomed at all times.

A mother caring for a litter of baby pups was a good life lesson in love and devotion to offspring.

The Metro Daily News

FINAL EDITION

MAY 8, 1945

V-E DAY
(VICTORY IN EUROPE)
Nazi Germany surrenders.

This *Post* cover features the makings of a boy's room complete with ball glove, baseball, fishing gear and darts game.

Bathing the family dog in an old wash tub was always a good activity for a hot summer afternoon, especially if the children got as wet as the dog.

Assembling homemade toys was a creative way of learning how to fix simple items around the house.

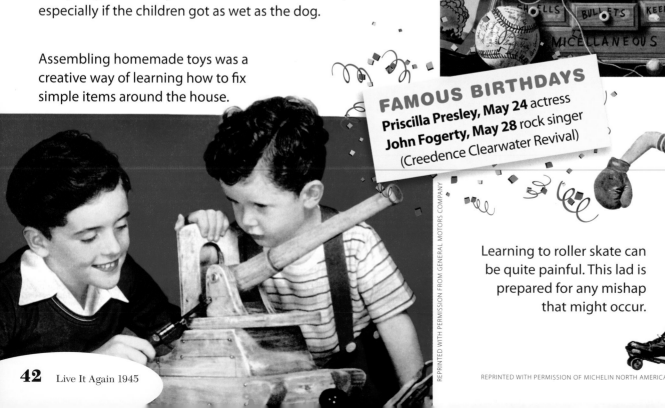

FAMOUS BIRTHDAYS
Priscilla Presley, May 24 actress
John Fogerty, May 28 rock singer
(Creedence Clearwater Revival)

Learning to roller skate can be quite painful. This lad is prepared for any mishap that might occur.

Everyday Life

To be a kid again

Memories of childhood in 1945 were often shaped by what kids heard on the radio, observed in comic books or read about in storybooks. Backyard playgrounds often expanded into western plains action and homemade baseball diamonds utilized rags, stones and boards for bases. Self-made football fields often included tall trees substituting as goal posts.

Blankets thrown over chairs or clotheslines became tents. Sometimes, young campers would take crackers, cookies and milk into their homemade shelters for consumption during self-appointed club meetings. Evenings were often spent listening to serial radio programs while eating popcorn or rich fudge candies.

Other games such as hopscotch led the way for activities utilizing neighborhood walks and driveways.

Household goods such as thread and buttons proved to be excellent materials for making necklaces and bracelets.

The coming of toys imitating science equipment such as microscopes and telescopes proved to be learning tools as well as fun for inquisitive young people.

Even the family pet joined a football game that ended up in the neighbor's pile of leaves.

Everyday Life

Family time

Closeness in family dynamics was the bond of hope and faith that enabled both those at home and overseas to have strength during wartime separation. Helping Dad with projects and listening to Grandpa talk about family legends drew siblings and parents closer together.

Parents made bathtime fun with special toys and methods of washing hair. Each family member was assigned chores that brought about a sense of teamwork. The evening meal was then utilized to talk over the day's activities. The words of each person were considered important and of personal worth.

The coming of a new baby added a sense of joy and an opportunity to teach responsibilities and acceptance among family members.

Bath time was a soothing time of fulfillment for Mother as she cared for her children.

"Now, Freddie, suppose you just slip into this little, old strait jacket."

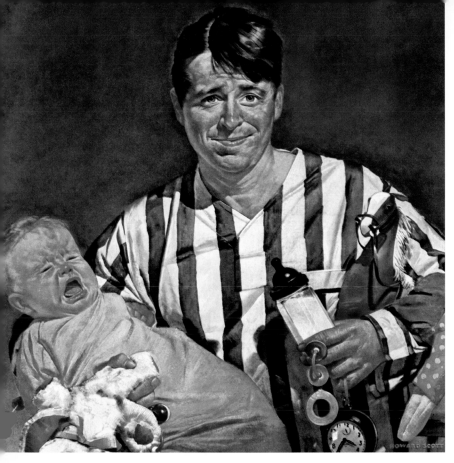

Love was often filled with exasperation when Dad could do nothing to satisfy a screaming child.

Story time was an important time of bonding and learning. It was an important tool of creative imagination before bedtime.

Introducing a new baby to family siblings was an important moment in learning life's lessons of sharing.

Family prayer was an important source of strength for all aspects of family life.

Family members often brought baby animals inside the home, especially during brutal winter nights.

Monday was often wash day. A good brisk breeze was always an asset in drying clothes hung on the clothesline.

Everyone gathered when it was time to harvest maple syrup in early spring.

Country Living

Country living was a merging of nature and man in ways unknown to those living in the cities. From the time they could carry a hoe, children worked in gardens, gathered eggs, milked cows and helped with food provision for the entire family.

Lessons in nature such as approaching storms, harvest, soil maintenance and caring for plants taught patterns that aided skills for a lifetime. Because chores were often shared, the togetherness enabled family members to share and experience common realities that were both fun and educational.

For many, the ringing of the dinner bell in the evening meant time for an evening meal consisting of meat, potatoes, vegetables and a homemade dessert. Suppertime was always the time of day where family members exchanged ideas and told of their experiences for the day.

JOHN FALTER

© 1945 SEPS

Caring for baby chicks was a bonding time for parents and children.

© 1945 SEPS

Country Living

Western style

Country living in the west took on a different countenance than it did in the east. It often involved severe weather changes which required sheltering cattle and making sure children arrived home from one-room schools. Sudden blizzards occasionally required students to stay at the school for a few days.

Rodeo competition was bred into the life of ranchers. The annual gathering of cattle, horses, cowboys and youthful competitors was often the event of the year in western towns.

Due to the size of ranches and distance from settlements, family trips were often made on a monthly basis to the closest urban center to stock up on goods to sustain life on the prairies. This meant extra planning for food and medical supplies for family members and livestock.

Ranchers worked all year preparing for the county rodeo each summer.

The vastness of the ranchland demanded careful tracking of the herds. Sometimes ranch hands could be on the range for days taking care of the cattle.

THE WEATHER
City and State—Hula,
Snow, Colder
Heate n Sale Almanac

The Metro Daily News

FINAL
EDITION

VOLUME 87 — No. 164
THE JOHNSTON PRESS

78 PAGES
FIVE CENTS

JUNE 30, 1945

SEVENTEEN-DAY NEWSPAPER STRIKE IN NEW YORK CITY BEGINS

Caring for the cattle often involved transporting bales of hay to the site where they were roaming, especially during bad weather.

Vast beauty and variation of scenery drew many adventurers to the western states.

The local saloon was a good place to take a breather and catch up with fellow ranchers about the latest news and trends of the farmland.

What Made Us Laugh

"First, tell me—is this coming out of the house money or are you treating us to dinner?"

"Maybe we'd better go someplace else for you to hear what I have to say, Elsie."

"We have room for two of your party!"

"Dearest, I'll sit here so I can look at you!"

"After this maybe you'll call and find out ahead of time whose band is playing during the dinner hour!"

"You had a phone call—I believe I'm gonna like him!"

"This one is frightfully expensive, madam—you're paying for restraint."

Hundreds of thousands of people came out to watch the 10 women's teams play.

Catchers were well-protected with pads and face gear. Left to right, Dottie Green and Nellie Nelson. The character played by Geena Davis in the 1996 movie *A League of Their Own* was loosely based on Dottie Green.

Players were not afraid to slide in to base, despite resulting scrapes and bruises.

Like their male counterparts, the girls sometimes argued with the umpire, but unlike the men, each player received a beauty kit complete with instructions.

Skirts in the Dirt

A new professional baseball league was formed in 1943 with women players. The idea was to maintain baseball in the public eye while most able men were away. In 1945, the All-American Girls Baseball League (AAGBL) was owned by chewing gum mogul Phillip Wrigley, and initial tryouts were held at Wrigley Field in Chicago.

The first players wore bloomers, but owners soon noticed people loved to see leg revealing uniforms. The players were then outfitted in short, flashy skirts that also increased mobility. During spring training, the girls were required to attend evening charm school classes. The girls were not permitted to have short hair, smoke or drink in public places, and were required to wear lipstick at all times. Following these rules was a small price to pay to achieve the highest position in the sport.

Connie Wisniewski, a Grand Rapids Chicks pitcher, was honored as the 1945 Player of the Year.

The Rockford Peaches were the All-American Girls Baseball League champions of 1945.

During the singing of the national anthem, a team forms the "V" for victory in honor of those who were serving in the military during World War II.

Players, ages 15 to 25, attended the required charm school held during spring training.

The local roller-skating rink made a nice place for a casual date on the weekends.

Recreational Fun

Some of the favorite memories of recreational life in 1945 involved simple fun and lots of time enjoying friends and family. Sunday afternoons were often spent with a carry-in dinner in the country followed by an afternoon of croquet, often topped off with homemade ice cream.

Music of the times serenaded young couples enjoying a fun evening at the roller skating rink. Bowling was a popular indoor game, sometimes slowed a bit while the pin spotters set up the next frame. On the inside, Ping-Pong caught the fancy of youth and those young at heart.

In the evenings or rainy afternoons, reading was still a popular pastime. Such novels as *Dick Tracy, Earth and High Heaven, Captain from Castile, So Well Remembered* and *The Black Rose* captured the attention of those looking for a literary escape during hard times.

1945 ARMSTRONG CORK COMPANY

A well-maintained croquet court attracted a crowd on balmy summer afternoons.

© LIBRARY OF CONGRESS, PRINTS AND PHOTOGRAPHS DIVISION, MATPC.12674

ng-Pong was often a good
ther-son activity. Dad usually
revailed with his knowledge of spins
om a game he experienced as a boy.

Bowling was a good hometown activity filled with the intense
competition of league play. Frames of pins were set up by hand and
the ball was delivered down a shoot by a retrieving individual.

A round of golf was often a good opportunity to chat
with friends while getting a bit of exercise.

Sprinkling cans and water hoses were a good way t play and keep cool with neighborhood friends.

FAMOUS BIRTHDAYS
Ron Glass, July 10 actor
Jim Davis, July 28 cartoonist

The courthouse square was a popular spot to gather for games, picnics and a parade on the Fourth of July. Downtown street fairs also provided opportunities to meet friends and enjoy carnival rides together.

The Chris-Craft Express Cruiser brought lots of enjoyment for those taking leisure boat rides on hot summer days.

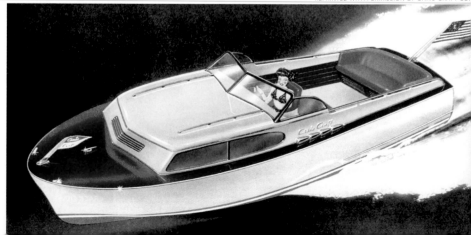

Recreational Fun

Lazy days of summer

The closest stream and swimming hole were popular spots of recreation on hot summer afternoons. Those fortunate enough to live close to an ocean or lake would often gather for sun bathing, games in the sand and an occasional splash in the waves. More private streams or rivers often provided solace for a quick moment of skinny dipping. Sometimes, those coming out of the water were surprised to find that their clothes had disappeared or ended in the top of some tree while they were in the water.

Community festivals were always a popular time to see friends and catch up on the latest news. Backyard activities ranged from playing sandlot baseball to running through sprinklers. Father and son outings such as fishing in a rowboat created memories for a lifetime.

Rowing to a good fishing spot was always a popular activity for those gathering at a neighborhood pond.

THE SATURDAY EVENING

POST

AUGUST 11, 1945   10¢

norman rockwell

A remote swimming hole provided a good place to dive in and cool off with a moment of skinny dipping.

Sporting Champions

In 1945, Byron Nelson won the PGA championship and was the PGA money tour leader with total earnings of $63,336 for the year. Several major tournaments, such as the Masters and U.S. Open, were not played because of the war.

In professional football, the Cleveland Rams defeated the Washington Redskins 15–14 to capture the National Football League Championship. After the season was over, the Rams relocated in Los Angeles. In baseball, the Detroit Tigers won the World Series.

Because of the events of World War II there were only two world championship boxing bouts in 1945. Willie Pep retained his world Featherweight title with a 15 round decision over Phil Terranova. Ike Williams won the Lightweight title, knocking out champion Juan Zurita in two rounds at Mexico City.

Famous actress Jane Russell poised on her knees after holding the football for husband Bob Waterfield, Cleveland Rams' star quarterback as he practices at the Cleveland Municipal Stadium.

Byron Nelson of Cleveland, Ohio, is being presented with the cup emblematic of his victory in the Professional Golf Association tournament at Dayton, Ohio. Runner-up Sammy Byrd is shown at far left with Ed Dudley, PGA president, in the center.

...y two world championships were ...ght in 1945 due to World War II. ...Featherweight and Lightweight ...s were still fought in the midst of ...time limitations.

The Detroit Tigers beat the Chicago Cubs in the sixth inning of the fifth World Series baseball game played in Chicago.

The Metro Daily News

FINAL EDITION

JULY 28, 1945

A U.S. ARMY AIR FORCES B-25 BOMBER FLIES INTO THE EMPIRE STATE BUILDING, KILLING 13

What Made Us Laugh

"Dear Mr. Sinatra: Father is furious about what you said during the presidential campaign and made me tear up all your pictures. But believe me, Mr. Sinatra, politics shall never destroy my feeling for you …"

"And it comes in three convenient sizes—small, which we have discontinued because of a shortage of materials; medium, which is still going to the armed forces; and large, which you can try and get."

"Oh, for heaven's sake! A ball game."

"We'll try to get back early, mother; however, we brought you a few extra things just in case."

"Nice crowd tonight! I wonder if Lunt and Fontanne can pack 'em in as we do?"

"Anybody seen the paper?"

"I'll have a Shopper's Special and my buddy here wants a Businessman's Lunch."

"Been practicing your bird calls again, dear?"

The Philco Radio-Phonograph was introduced featuring an automatic record player. Users just inserted a record in the slot and it played.

REPRINTED WITH PERMISSION OF PHILIPS COMPANY ARCHIVES

1945 BITUMINOUS COAL INSTITUTE

Televisions were available, but were still too expensive for the majority of Americans.

Radio Stars & Hits of 1945

Adventures of Ellery Queen

Amos 'n' Andy

Bing Crosby

Captain Midnight

Edgar Bergen & Charlie McCarthy

Fibber McGee & Molly

Green Hornet

Lone Ranger

Mr. Keen, Tracer of Lost Persons

Sherlock Holmes

Smilin' Ed's Buster Brown Gang

Suspense

Tommy Dorsey Orchestra

The Metro Daily News

FINAL EDITION

THE WEATHER

VOLUME 67 — No. 181

AUGUST 15, 1945

V-J DAY
(VICTORY OVER JAPAN)
Emperor Hirohito announces Japan's surrender.

That's Entertainment

Radio & Television

During 1945, radio reigned as the king of entertainment. Families gathered around the radio to listen to *Amos 'n' Andy*, a very popular nightly comedy set in the African/American community. *Fibber McGee & Molly* and *The Bob Hope Show* continued to get good ratings. Bing Crosby sang such music hits as "You Belong to My Heart" while Frank Sinatra crooned "You'll Never Walk Alone." Televisions were expensive and development was put on hold until after World War II. In 1945 there were fewer than 7,000 television sets in the country and only nine stations on the air.

"Take that, you arch-fiend, and that and that!"

Philco, one of the leading radio manufacturers, brought the latest developments for modern enjoyment of radio and recorded music.

Ellery Queen, writer of detective fiction, is pictured with Marian Shockley, with whom he enacted some of his mystery stories over the radio.

That's Entertainment

Singers & Bands

In 1945, people were still dancing to the enormously popular sounds of the swing bands, but wartime travel restrictions made it tough for big groups to travel freely. Singers then began to take center stage. Vaughn Monroe was one of the popular male vocalists to come out of the big-band phenomenon. Many a young couple fell in love to Monroe's crooning of some sentimental melody.

Songs from the movies often became big hits, but no other movie star of the era had as much crossover success as Bing Crosby. His hit "White Christmas", from the movie of the same title, became a favorite Christmas song for generations to come. The singing Andrews Sisters were a part of everyone's life during World War II.

© GETTY IMAGES

Above, American actress and singer Doris Day sang to the accompaniment of American jazz musician Les Brown and his band. A favorite pastime was listening to favorite songs and dancing the lindy, a form of jitterbug.

Top Hits of 1945

"Rum & Coca-Cola"
Andrews Sisters

"Till the End of Time"
Perry Como

"Sentimental Journey"
Les Brown

"On the Atchison, Topeka and the Santa Fe"
Johnny Mercer

"My Dreams Are Getting Better"
Les Brown

"I Can't Begin to Tell You"
Bing Crosby

"There! I've Said It Again"
Vaughn Monroe

"Chickery Chick"
Sammy Kaye

"White Christmas"
Bing Crosby

"It's Been a Long, Long Time"
Bing Crosby

...ughn Monroe, big band leader, played the trombone as he ...formed onstage. He also became a well-known vocalist ...h his rich baritone voice.

Upon their arrival back in the states, returning soldiers are entertained by the Andrews Sisters in New York City. These sisters were America's most popular female singing group.

THE SCREEN DARES TO OPEN THE STRANGE AND SAVAGE PAGES OF A SHOCKING BEST-SELLER!

"THE LOST WEEK-END"

From the Novel by CHARLES JACKSON

Paramount's Sensation Starring

RAY MILLAND JANE WYMAN

with PHILLIP TERRY · HOWARD da SILVA · DORIS DOWLING · FRANK FAYLEN · Produced by CHARLES BRACKETT · Directed by BILLY WILDER · Screen Play by Charles Brackett and Billy Wilder

The Lost Weekend won four Oscars—Best Picture, Best Director (Billy Wilder), Best Actor (Ray Milland) and Best Screenplay.

That's Entertainment

The silver screen

At the conclusion of World War II, the government ended restrictions on allocation of film stock and bans on outdoor lighting displays, allowing more freedom for the movie industry. *The Lost Weekend* drama about the desperate life of a chronic alcoholic won best picture at the Academy Awards and top prize at the Cannes Film Festival. *The Bells of St. Mary's* was the second highest grossing film, starring Bing Crosby and Ingrid Bergman. "Aren't You Glad You're You" was an Oscar nominee for Best Original Song.

Joan Crawford, with a reputation for being difficult, surprised everyone by delivering one of the best performances of her career in *Mildred Pierce*. *Anchor's Away* featured Gene Kelly famously dancing with Jerry, the mouse cartoon character. This was one of the first times live action was combined with animation.

Zachary Scott, Ann Blyth and Joan Crawford in the film *Mildred Pierce*. Ms. Crawford won best actress for her leading role as a loving mother to an ungrateful daughter.

Cornel Wilde and actress Gene Tierney are shown in a scene from *Leave Her to Heaven* in which Ms. Tierney was nominated as Best Actress for her role. The movie won an Oscar for Best Cinematography.

© GETTY IMAGES

Tops at the Box Office

Mom and Dad
The Bells of St. Mary's
Leave Her to Heaven
Spellbound
Anchors Aweigh
The Dolly Sisters
Week-End at the Waldorf
Mildred Pierce
The Lost Weekend
Saratoga Trunk
Diamond Horseshoe
The Valley of Decision

AMOUS BIRTHDAYS
oni Anderson, August 5 actress
teve Martin, August 14 actor and comedian

Father O'Malley (Bing Crosby) sings with Sister Benedict (Ingrid Bergman) in *The Bells of St. Mary's*. In the film, the two indulge in a friendly rivalry and succeed in helping to extend a Catholic school. Ms. Bergman won the Golden Globe for Best Actress.

Mail by the ton was shipped on planes to various parts of the world and the United States during World War II.

Packages from home took lots of sorting to distribute to troops fighting in the war. Christmastime was always the busiest for the postal workers.

The Mail Gets Through

The exchange of mail during World War II was such a heart-felt activity that many veterans and those they corresponded with saved their letters for the rest of their lives.

For many, letters from home was the only way of hearing about loved ones, happenings and receiving encouragement from family and friends. In America, relatives and friends often ran to the mailbox immediately after the mail arrived to look for updates on their loved ones serving in the military.

Romances were sustained and kindled through correspondence. In some cases, girls who sent letters of encouragement to servicemen later became brides when their man returned home.

One of the most endearing exchanges was between military personnel and Mother, whose sensitive words to children at war brought comfort and strength to their hearts. Mail time was always the highlight of the day at camp sites in foreign lands.

Many times the military personnel delivering the mail were placed in harm's way, but the mail had to get through to our troops.

© 1945 SEPS

Love letters were a time of reflection and sometimes tears. Letters between those in love served as glaring reminders of the distance between them, while comforting the hearts of those waiting to hear.

REPRINTED WITH
PERMISSION OF
ASSOCIATION OF
AMERICAN RAILROADS

Lines of eager troops formed during mail call after postal service arrived from America.

REPRINTED WITH PERMISSION FROM HONEYWELL INTERNATIONAL

U.S. ARMY SIGNAL CORPS

Rest and Relaxation Military Style

To boost morale of the troops, Gen. Eisenhower instigated a plan for time off the battlefield. Usually for 48 hours, European-front soldiers as many as 2,000 at a time, were taken by truck to Paris. Only Allied soldiers who actually endured the hardships and danger of combat were eligible. Staying in luxurious hotel rooms, GIs ate delicious French-cooked meals, went sightseeing, danced at night in clubs and took as many hot baths as they wanted. No trip to Paris was complete without a visit to the Eiffel Tower. One soldier said, "I never saw so many pretty girls in all my life."

In Australia, soldiers serving on the Pacific Front visited Brisbane's zoo to pet the wallabies and kangaroos. Brisbane's Botanical Gardens reminded Americans of home with bands that played on Sunday afternoons. Male officers, as was the case all over the world, entertained the ladies at officers' clubs. Swimming in Australia's warm waters was a simple way to relax. Troops returned by truck to the battlefield refreshed, sharing wisecracks and banter.

Free time was essential for troop morale. GIs relaxed in Paris cafés and watched the mademoiselles go by. Lack of gas prompted a change from traditional taxis to bicycle conveyances. Evenings were spent dining and dancing.

U.S. ARMY SIGNAL CORPS

Coming home was the ultimate form of rest and relaxation.

Public payphones in Brisbane, Australia, were in street booths. Americans had to get the hang of a different pay system.

Women's Army Corps (WAC) swimmers enjoying a lift on an amphibious truck in New Guinea. Presence of these girls emphasized how secure Australia had become.

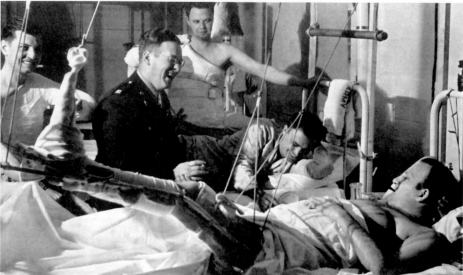

Chaplain Hoffman visits wounded soldiers, who noticeably brighten up during his stay.

Kindness reaches across the barriers of war as soldiers interacted with the children of other nations.

The Red Cross funded and distributed parcels and medical kits for American prisoners of war.

The Metro Daily News

FINAL EDITION

THE WEATHER
City and State—Fair,
Snow, Colder

VOLUME 67—No. 161

FIVE CENTS

SEPTEMBER 2, 1945

WORLD WAR II ENDS

The final official surrender of Japan is accepted by the Supreme Allied Commander, General Douglas MacArthur and Fleet Admiral Chester Nimitz for the United States.

Sharing Kind Acts

The International Red Cross continued to be the war icon of compassion. United States men and women volunteered their time and prepared bandages for first-aid kits, visited wounded servicemen in hospitals and collected blood for them. The volunteers also distributed magazines, coffee and other small comforts to soldiers headed overseas as well as to POW camps. To the troops, a Red Cross package from home was a symbol of being remembered.

Though bird-dogging of the wounded was not a part of a chaplain's job, one man made it his front-line specialty. Beloved army chaplain Albert Hoffman was remembered by many for his selfless acts of kindness to the wounded and dying. He stuck with the foot soldiers, encouraging and carrying items from overloaded gunners' packs. He later was awarded the Silver Star and Purple Heart in recognition of his efforts.

Some relations that developed during the war lasted a lifetime. Editor Barb Sprunger's father, Gorman McKean, and a few Army buddies were befriended by the Fred Bridges family of England. The soldiers frequently visited the home of the couple and their young daughter, Mavis. After the war, the McKean and Bridges families remained in contact and even visited each other.

© 1945 SEPS

Right, bomber crews were met by a Red Cross girl with refreshments. Upper right is soldier Gorman McKean who was befriended by the parents of young English girl, Mavis Bridges, shown below.

Advances in Medicine

Wartime needs led to advances in medical technology. In earlier wars, many wounded soldiers died from infections. During the latter years of World War II, army medics depended on penicillin to treat the soldiers. Penicillin was a wonder drug that fought bacterial infections throughout the body. Tens of thousands of servicemen survived wounds that would otherwise have killed them.

The army had other reasons to be grateful to scientists. Troops fighting in the jungles of the South Pacific frequently came down with malaria, a deadly tropical illness transmitted by mosquitoes. When scientists achieved a laboratory-formed version of quinine, they discovered it was more effective in fighting malaria than natural quinine. United States chemists also fought malaria through the development of insecticides such as DDT.

Before the discovery of X-ray in 1895, medical diagnosis could prove difficult. By World War II, the X-ray machine was thoroughly incorporated into American society. The machine was improved by leaps and bounds; images became clearer, the process safer for both patient and technician. It became portable and easier to use.

Control laboratories were vital spots in the production of all medications, because their proper action depended on accurate control of quality. In its mission of healing, the antibiotic penicillin lifted many more sick and wounded back to hope and health.

FAMOUS BIRTHDAYS
Jose Feliciano, September 10
Puerto Rican singer
Phil Jackson, September 17
basketball coach

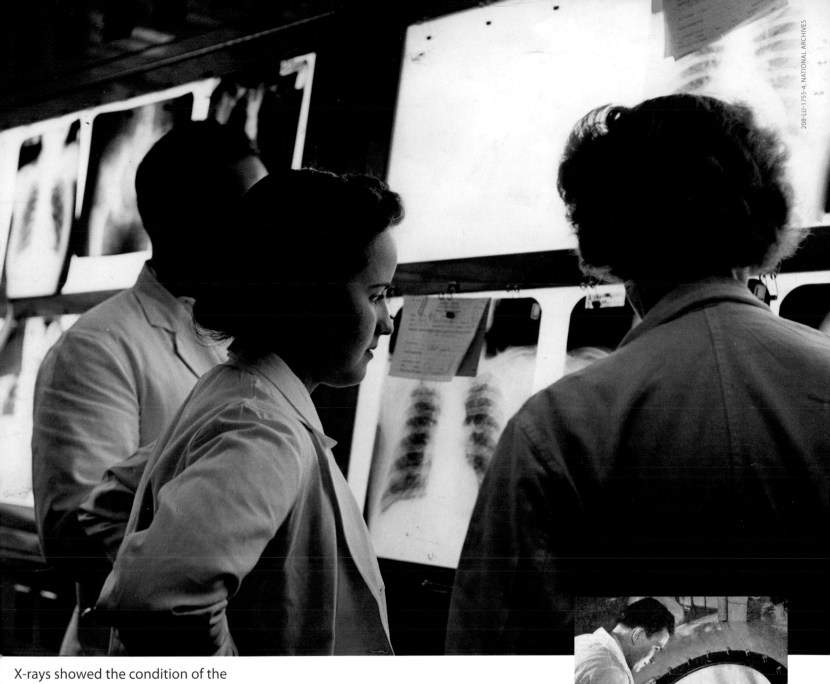

X-rays showed the condition of the patient before operating. Advancements opened the door for many women to take their places in medical professions formerly open only to men.

Looking down into one of the giant tanks at a penicillin plant where tens of thousands of gallons of penicillin culture broth was incubated every 48 hours. Through new technology, penicillin was produced in much larger quantities.

The Common Cold

We stay out of drafts, drink plenty of liquids, avoid crowds, and what happens? In spite of every precaution almost all of us sooner or later come down with a common cold. In these sketches published in the *Post* Jan. 1945 issue, Norman Rockwell shows that this uncommonly annoying affliction succeeds in ruffling our dignity and spoiling our fun. No matter how many advances we discover in the world of medicine, we still have to fight "The Common Cold."

There are times when you can't let a cold upset you!

Many germ strategists prescribe the direct frontal attack.

He promised to love, honor and ah-choo! A faithful wife must share his flu.

Officer Clancy needs no whistle. When he says "Stob!" he means "Dode go."

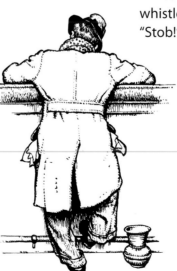

A head cold today— A head tomorrow!

The all-out remedy for the patient who is all in.

How your head feels in that first 24 hours.

It looks as though Reverend Fernum will end his sermon with the usual "Let us spray."

The professor welcomes the chance to curl up with some good bacilli.

An appreciative audience, the right acoustics, and he's off.

The only thing worse than a cold is what Ma gives you to prevent it.

No dance. No date. No fun. Cheer up! It could have been no tissues!

Be patriotic and keep it under your hat. Anyhow— is this trip necessary?

The tub treatment relaxes the patient while drowning the germs.

Victory in Sight

War in Europe

In early February, as Allied forces closed in on the German heartland, their political leaders met at Yalta in the Soviet Union to plan the war's end and aftermath. Two days after the conference, British and American bombers devastated the German city of Dresden. While the bombers were at work, British and American ground troops had broken free from where they had been bottled up by the Battle of the Bulge. The Rhine River was the last formidable barrier in western Germany. The Germans retreating across the Rhine blew up every bridge but one, at Remagen, Germany. When troops rode into town, they were astonished to find the bridge still standing. Two weeks later, at Oppenheim, Germany, Patton's Third Army sneaked across the river at night in assault boats. On April 12, the day President Roosevelt died, fast-moving United States tanks drove near Berlin, meeting the Soviets.

Gen. Eisenhower along with Lt. Generals Patton, Bradley and Hodges share a light-hearted moment of laughter.

Soldiers of the 347th Infantrymen Regiment stand in line for food rations during the bitter cold of winter.

The 55th Armored Infantry Battalion and tank of the 22nd Tank Battalion advance on the streets of Wernberg, Germany.

When they pile out of the truck, this load of replacements, newly assigned to combat outfits and stripped to the bare essentials of living and fighting, will be at the battle front.

A replacement gets into his "Long Johns". A foxhole, even when the days are mild, can be mighty cold at night.

gineers named the bridge they built over the Sûre River, connecting Luxemburg to Germany, Gen. Patton. Some disliked him, but most of his troops idolized "the old so-and-so".

A jubilant American soldier hugs an English woman and victory smiles light the faces of happy servicemen and civilians at Piccadilly Circus, London, celebrating Germany's unconditional surrender on May 7, 1945.

On April 22, 1945, American troops paraded in Nuremberg Stadium, the location of many Nazi political rallies. The United States flag was proudly draped over the Swastika symbol.

Troops leave the battlegrounds via trucks. The war in Europe was over, the time for rebuilding had begun.

Victory in Sight

War ends in Europe

Following the 1944 D-Day Allied invasion in Normandy, France, directed by U.S. Gen. Dwight D. Eisenhower, Hitler poured all the remaining strength of his army into western Europe. By April 1945, it appeared that an Allied victory was imminent. German resistance weakened quickly under the assault of swift moving Allied armies. On May 7, 1945, Germany signed an unconditional surrender, bringing an end to the war in Europe. Americans celebrated and kissing strangers was a common reaction to the news. Millions of people joined parades to welcome home troops and American generals. American faith in the future had been reborn and the United States emerged from the conflict as the most powerful nation on earth.

Above: On May 7, 1945, Gen. Alfred Jodl, Chief of the Operations Staff in the German High Command, signs the document of unconditional German surrender in Reims, France. Below: Allied forces leaders, including Gen. Eisenhower (center), shown holding pens shaped in a "V" for victory, attend the signing.

On April 25, 1945, American troops coming from the west met up with Soviet forces coming from the east in Torgau (Saxon, Germany).

Troops receiving last minute instructions before an air attack mission.

Battles for the islands near Japan were fiercely fought, making them the most costly operations in Marine Corps history, claiming many lives.

Victory in Sight

War in the Pacific

Iwo Jima, a tiny island 660 miles south of Tokyo, was considered vital to the war with Japan. United States ships and planes gave Iwo Jima the heaviest pre-invasion pounding of the Pacific war. But when the first marines landed, they found the enemy nearly unharmed and holed up in bunkers and caves connected by 11 miles of tunnels. The marines clawed their way to victory at the summit as shown in the famous photo on the facing page.

Okinawa, the last island stepping-stone to Japan, offered more of the familiar enemy fanaticism. The Japanese prepared to defend this island less than 350 miles from their homeland with the most massive attacks of kamikaze suicide planes so far. On April 1, in the largest amphibious operation of the Pacific war, United States troops landed on Okinawa. The Japanese were so well entrenched that the invaders would have to pay dearly for every inch, but an end to the war was in sight.

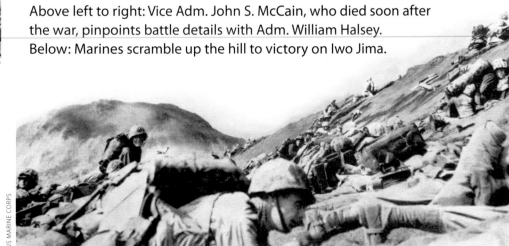

Above left to right: Vice Adm. John S. McCain, who died soon after the war, pinpoints battle details with Adm. William Halsey.
Below: Marines scramble up the hill to victory on Iwo Jima.

ENOLA GAY

President Truman announces Japan's surrender Aug. 14, 19

Col. Paul W. Tibbets, Jr., pilot of the *Enola Gay*, the plane that dropped the atomic bomb on Hiroshima, waves from his cockpit before takeoff.

The *Post* was the first and only publication to publish photographer Larry Keighley's photograph of the Japanese surrender aboard the battleship *USS Missouri* in Tokyo Bay. In the foreground, Gen. Yoshijiro Umezu is signing the surrender terms for the Japanese. On the Japanese general's right, opposite side of table, is Lt. Gen. Sutherland, Gen. MacArthur's Chief of Staff. Back of the microphone stands Gen. MacArthur.

Victory in Sight

War ends in the Pacific

On Aug. 6, a B-29 bomber took off from the island of Tinian and dropped an atomic bomb on the Japanese city of Hiroshima. The bomb carried the destructive power of 20,000 tons of regular explosive. Most of the city vanished in a single blinding flash. President Truman called on Japan to surrender or face "a rain of ruin from the air." Yet the Japanese government refused.

On Aug. 9, the United States dropped a second atomic bomb on Nagasaki. Japan's emperor finally asked his government to seek peace. News of Japan's surrender was announced by President Truman on Aug. 14—V-J Day (Victory over Japan Day). Americans went wild with joy. Huge crowds gathered everywhere to celebrate and strangers hugged and kissed.

New York City celebrating the surrender of Japan. They threw anything and kissed strangers in Times Square. This photo became an icon of the victory.

The mushroom-shaped cloud of destruction billows upward from the atomic bomb dropped on Nagasaki.

1945 MOTOR BUS LINES OF AMERICA

Bringing Home the Troops

Soldiers coming home from World War II were greeted with excitement and heralded as heroes. Family members and friends met their loved ones at train stations waving banners and signs with their names on them. For those returning by ship, the sight of the Statue of Liberty in New York Harbor brought instant tears.

A large number of troops were commissioned to return to the United States following the surrender of Japan. Many sailed underneath the Golden Gate Bridge just before they reached American soil. It wasn't unusual for those arriving to kiss the ground or break into tears when they arrived at home in the United States.

A train was waiting near the transport ship to carry troops to the train stations closest to their homes.

Those arriving from Europe were overwhelmed when they first glimpsed the Statue of Liberty at the entrance of New York Harbor.

The first step for some beginning their return to America came through this bomb-scarred Italian port where walking wounded and ambulance cases assembled joyously to board a Coast Guard-manned transport.

FAMOUS BIRTHDAYS
John Lithgow, October 19 actor
Henry Winkler, October 30 actor

Warm hugs and tearful embraces filled the arms of lovers who had been apart during the war.

Children ran and leaped into the arms of their fathers as they walked through the front door to the excited screams of a family who loved them.

Welcome Home!

Oh! The excitement of coming home; the moment all military personnel and their families and friends had been waiting for since they entered the service.

The last few miles before home were usually the toughest for many servicemen who were eagerly looking forward to seeing their families and loved ones. Many soldiers hitchhiked from the bus stations to their hometown communities. Some walked the last few miles during the night in adverse weather in order to arrive sooner on the doorsteps of those they loved.

Those arriving often felt dazed initially. After the horrors of war, it was difficult for them to believe that it was past them and they were back with their families. They were home and that was all that mattered.

Jubilation and tears broke out at all hours of the day as soldiers were welcomed by family and friends.

The Metro Daily News

FINAL EDITION

OCTOBER 5, 1945

HOLLYWOOD BLACK FRIDAY

A strike between the set decorators' union and the studio results in a riot.

For many, the return home meant being welcomed by an excited wife or girlfriend. Mother's prayers were answered when her son was finally in sight.

Back to Civilian Life

The return of American troops following the end of World War II was both a time of carefree happiness and changes in lifestyle. Servicemen who had been in peril on the battlefield often had recurring nightmares from their experiences. They were often in awe of the changes in family members and needed to adjust to the American way of life.

Many women who served as soldiers returned to their families. Mom, Dad and children adjusted to changes in family dynamics that had prevailed while their loved one was gone. Family members worked to adjust to a new world view brought home by those who had been in war in a different culture. Friends and loved ones gathered with an eagerness to hear what the returning veterans were willing to share.

Returning soldiers enjoyed the company of friends once again. Soldiers were interested in hearing about new tools and economic changes that occurred while they were gone. Those at home wanted to hear the story of war.

Children enjoyed stepping into their father's shoes temporarily to wear war clothes and listen to stories of military duty.

Many women who worked in manufacturing plants found themselves back in the office.

THE SATURDAY EVENING

POST

DECEMBER 15, 1945   10¢

Beginning:

MY THREE YEARS WITH EISENHOWER

THE INTIMATE DIARY
OF THE GENERAL'S AIDE
Capt. HARRY BUTCHER, USNR

Norman Rockwell

Many returning soldiers found their clothes to be the wrong size upon their return home. Younger soldiers entered the service as boys, but returned as men.

A horseback ride could be turned into a romantic interlude.

Cold weather brought new dating possibilities, such as skimming across t ice hand in hand.

Fishing for the big one was much more exciting with a certain companion.

Soldiers missed their cars, and being home again brought freedom to dating.

In the Mood for Love

The courtship

During the war, America had a job to do. All able-bodied men were involved in military efforts and women were preoccupied with supporting the servicemen in all possible ways. Once peace reigned again, thoughts returned to having fun and dating. Romance was in the air and opportunities for dates abounded. Returning soldiers reclaimed their cars and gas was no longer rationed. Dates did not have to be expensive. Couples spent many pleasant evenings listening to the latest radio shows, fishing and going on picnics in the sunshine. Simple pleasures were relished after the hard times of war.

© 1945 SEPS

"Boy! Did I look forward to this!"

In the Mood for Love

The wedding

After the separation and anxiety of war, couples simply wanted to be together. Many couples were in a hurry to be married, which did not allow time for planning elaborate weddings. There were over 1.6 million wedding ceremonies performed during 1945. Women often wore their best dresses in a variety of colors and men donned their military uniforms for quiet weddings at home, in a chapel or office of a justice of the peace. Others opted for longer engagements with more time for long white gowns, elaborate wedding cakes and a full guest list.

Gorman and Lorraine McKean were married during a furlough in 1945. He arrived home on a Tuesday and exactly one week later they were married in their pastor's home.

"Keep together, folks—we don't want no mix-ups."

Bakery businesses boomed along with the flood of weddings. Some weddings included punch and a beautifully decorated cake.

If time permitted, shopping for the perfect dress became enjoyable once again. Cloth was no longer rationed and flowing white wedding dresses reappeared.

1945 THE GENERAL TIRE

"I'm glad she finally got one of her own."

REPRINTED WITH PERMISSION OF PRUDENTIAL FINANCIAL, INC.

Glittering wedding rings symbolized a bright future for the couples who pledged to share for better or for worse, for richer or for poorer in 1945.

Couples proved you can have a grand honeymoon in your own home, provided you are in love and your mother-in-law doesn't show up.

Thanks to the GI Bill, veterans enjoyed access to low-interest housing loans and could afford a home, even though the furnishings were added slowly.

The Metro Daily News

THE WEATHER
City off Date—Rain.
Snow, Colder
Details in Extra Sections

FINAL
EDITION

VOLUME 97 — No. 161

30 PAGES

FIVE CENTS

NOVEMBER 16, 1945

MOTION PICTURE *THE LOST WEEKEND* IS RELEASED

This is the most realistic film portrayal of alcoholism up to this time.

In the Mood for Love

The newlyweds

Dreams were coming true for couples in 1945. Love had been found, the wedding knot was tied, and the honeymoon was the next memorable event. Newlywed couples tended to honeymoon a little closer to home due to gasoline prices and the fact that air travel was still in its infancy. Top destinations included Niagara Falls in New York, or a trip to the Pocono Mountains in Pennsylvania. No money for a conventional honeymoon? Many couples chose to honeymoon at home, where even the smallest details took on precious significance.

Once the rice had been cleared out of suitcases, the wonderful real living of a marriage began. Dreams extended to include hopes of a house of their own, but in reality, homes were in short supply, jumpstarting the largest housing boom in American history.

Women no longer needed to do the work of the men who had gone to war and could focus on home and hearth.

For newlyweds, there was joy in everyday activities.

A man's top priority was establishing a home and providing for his wife.

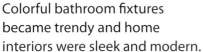

Colorful bathroom fixtures became trendy and home interiors were sleek and modern.

Our Homes

The great need for housing was met with an explosion of construction. The average asking price for a house in 1945 was about $4,600.00. Clean-lined housing designs were the top choice for the modern home. Housing options varied from practical to elegant. Rooms were thoughtfully arranged with sleeping quarters well removed from the noises of the living area. Many home exteriors were dressed up with the use of brick siding. High-contrast color schemes were in vogue, with pink and blue most popular for bedrooms and bathrooms, and brighter colors, such as red, for kitchens. It was thought work went more quickly in a cheerful kitchen.

What Made Us Laugh

"Try one, Charlie, they're delicious—just ask for a special cherry-marshmallow flip!"

"Sometimes I wish he would just howl like other dogs when she plays!"

The Parents Handbook by: Ethel Jacobson

Children are wonderful. Their motion is perpetual. I think they're an invention that is likely here to stay. Their rages are thunderful. Their smiles are King Cophetual. If patience is a virtue, it is not in their Roget. They lead the spryest parents by a couple of dozen jumps, and they're always having measles, and they're always having mumps.

But what's so adorable as children, camellia-like, Roseate and Dresdenish and dewy-eyed and such. Their manners are deplorable, their faces St. Cecilia-like. To any sort of home they add a decorative touch. They're pink-and-white bambinos in a della Robbia wreath. And they're always skinning noses, and they're always shedding teeth.

Yet children are durable. They're sturdy and they're muscular. They're really not a luxury, the wear and tear they take! Their energy's incurable. From dawn till it's crepuscular, they run and bounce and tumble till you wonder they don't break. Well, they do! With the gusto of a barrelful of lemurs, they're always smashing clavicles and fracturing their femurs.

Oh, there's nothing like an offspring to keep a home in foment. You may be bowed and bloody, but there's never a dull moment! There's times I'm moved to wonder how they get to ten alive. But mostly I just marvel that parents survive.

"I hate to mention this, Stamslowski, but I
think they're on to our signals."

"I'm going to ask you an important question, Mildred—
provided, of course, your term grades prove satisfactory."

"You certainly picked a fine cave for us to
hibernate in this winter!"

"I always dread the first few days after
she gets a manicure!"

In the News

The assembly of the world's first general purpose electronic computer—Electronic Numerical Integrator and Computer (ENIAC) was completed in 1945. After the war, production returned to domestic items in order to start pumping products back into America's economy. Slinky was created in Philadelphia by a shipbuilder working on a WW II battleship who accidently dropped a tension spring which gave the idea for the toy. The Slinky became an immediate top-seller at Gimbel's Department Store.

208-LU-38Z-2, NATIONAL ARCHIVES

REPRINTED WITH PERMISSION FROM THOMAS JAMES

Slinky inventor Richard James and son Thomas play with Slinkys on the stairs of the James home in Philadelphia in 1945. The toy immediately became a nationwide hit.

REPRINTED WITH PERMISSION FROM THOMAS JAMES

ok at the size of the ENIAC! It covered 1,800 feet of floor space. This huge computer was especially designed to calculate tillery firing tablets for the United States Arm's Ballistic Research Laboratory, but its first use was in calculations for the drogen bomb.

postwar radios off the assembly lines since war's end are ready for the public after the holidays. Employees from the Emerson Radio and Phonograph Corp. do their best to g a great product to eager customers.

Manufacturing Boom

Once American industry no longer needed to support an active war, manufacturers refocused their efforts back to the hometown economy. Steel that had been used in the manufacturing of warplanes became instrumental in the construction of commercial airlines for a worldwide market. New trains, cars, trucks, farm implements, household appliances and tools were quickly produced and put into the domestic market. The turnaround provided employment for returning soldiers.

Designers developed innovative ideas to produce electricity from coal to satisfy the growing power needs of companies expanding production lines. An immediate need developed to expand the oil industry due to the many auto industry purchases. Also, oil was becoming more popular in home heating where residents had once used wood and coal furnaces.

REPRINTED WITH PERMISSION FROM GENERAL MOTORS COMPANY

1945 BITUMINOUS COAL INSTITUTE

A work force of 204,000 employees supported 1,150 electric utility companies in their 24-hours-a-day effort to serve Americans. Their work helped sustain a steady flow of electric power for factories, farms and homes.

Soldiers who risked their lives during the war were given the opportunity to establish themselves for a future of industrial and financial stability for their families.

e oil industry continued to develop new technology to hance the nation's fuel industry and support the growing tomotive manufacturing efforts.

Automotive industrialists work together to plan the conversion of manufacturing war material to domestic product using 6-inch model machines.

Here they come!

1945 SUNBEAM PRODUCTS

"It's new…it's exclusive…it's PROCTOR"
…Coming soon!

Proctor Automatic Waffler makes waffles browned to your taste. Automatic glow cone signals when waffle is done.

Proctor Roast-or-Grille combines oven and grilling unit in convenient, portable form. Heavily insulated. Correct cooking temperatures controlled automatically. Easy to use.

The Proctor Never-Lift Iron …lifts itself and stands at the touch of a button. Legs snap back when ironing is resumed. Makes ironing easier and faster.

PROCTOR
AUTOMATIC ELECTRIC APPLIANCES

For efficient repairs, 105 service stations from coast to coast—see local classified phone book

PROCTOR ELECTRIC COMPANY, DIVISION OF PROCTOR & SCHWARTZ, INC., PHILADELPHIA 40, PENNSYLVANIA

PRINTED WITH PERMISSION OF HAMILTON BEACH

"Of course I'll need a maid. Yo don't think I can operate all the laborsaving devices myself?"

Manufacturing Boom

Home appliances

With the war ending, factories once again had the supplies needed for home appliances. Manufacturers could not make enough products at first to satisfy the pent-up demand. Production lines turned out sparkling new appliances with the last word in efficiency and convenience. Consumers enjoyed better living through handsome, modern refrigerators, washing machines and ranges. A wide range of small appliances also became available to make chores easier and faster, including the automatic waffler, electric roaster, never-lift iron and automatic toaster.

Companies raced to promote their products to consumers. Familiar brands emphasized dependability while new companies advertised convenience, touting advancements as being more efficient. Happy living was promoted as being attainable with the latest gadgets.

Vacuum cleaner business was booming, with demand far exceeding the supply.

Almost every American benefits every day from the products of **BORG-WARNER**

Manufacturers turned out large quantities of appliances to meet the high demand at the end of World War II.

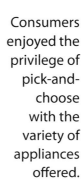

Consumers enjoyed the privilege of pick-and-choose with the variety of appliances offered.

Auto Industry Comes Alive

The end of the war brought excitement to a nation that had been anticipating changes in style and dependability of automobiles. Advertisements boasted of glamour, higher mileage, comfort and sturdiness. The auto industry stressed that experience gained in building war-time vehicles had provided insight for the development of better vehicles for our nation.

Ford Motor Company used such features as more power, safety and appearance to draw the attention of potential buyers. Cadillac advertised more improvements were made during the four years of war than would have been in four years of peace. General Motors vehicles were said to have made large advancements in mechanical improvements, while Nash was featured as a car that was easy to handle, fast accelerating and safe. Packard's advertisements stated buying a Packard Clipper was a "long haul" investment for the consumer.

Packard Clipper

Nash 600

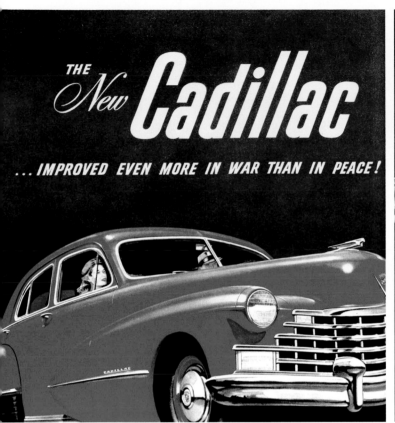

THE *New* **Cadillac**

... IMPROVED EVEN MORE IN WAR THAN IN PEACE!

Cadillac

Ford

Willys Jeep

DeSoto

Mercury

Auto Industry Comes Alive

Time to buy a new car

It had been four long years of not being able to purchase a new vehicle. Car owners were patching tires and continually fixing anything that went wrong with their vehicles since the war began. Surveys at the time indicated that a large portion of the population was considering the purchase of a new car once the war was over.

After the end of the war, car manufacturing didn't happen quickly enough for some potential buyers. Car orders were delayed due to material shortages and some manufacturers had to fulfill government contracts before converting back to civilian-car production. But the wait was worth it when one could finally own a new car.

Pontiac

Oldsmobile

Chevrolet

Traveling Again

All aboard! Many say these were the "glory days" of train travel. It's easy to see why, with air travel still in its infancy and car travel restricted by gas rationing. Trains were the preferred method of long-distance travel. Trains of the time were elegant with many amenities and staffed with porters, bartenders and waiters.

Air travel began to be promoted to usher in the new era of progress in air transportation. Airlines could fly more than 100 miles per hour faster than other transports. Swift, luxurious air travel was available at a cost lower than first-class railroad rates.

Bus operators led the way to all the scenic grandeur of America, keeping pace with the continuing development of America's highways. Buses were the most cost-effective service for those who couldn't travel otherwise. Travel was just around the "bend in the road" for millions of people.

MOTOR BUS LINES

1945 MOTOR BUS LINES OF AMERICA

Cruise ships, once popular among the rich and famous, were converted into troop carriers during the war.

Trains were glamorous and streamlined, complete with sleeper, dining and lounge cars.

Air travel was promoted as the most modern and speedy way to travel.

The Metro Daily News

FINAL EDITION

DECEMBER 20, 1945

ATIONING OF AUTO TIRES ENDS IN UNITED STATES

THE SATURDAY EVENING

POST

OCTOBER 20, 1945   **10¢**

What We Need is a
Good Three-Cent Air Line
By C. R. SMITH

**The Provocative
New Senator From Oregon**
By MARGARET THOMPSON

JOHN FALTER

© 1945 SEPS

Playing the piano for family
and friends was a favorite
Sunday afternoon activity.

FAMOUS BIRTHDAYS
Bette Midler, December 1 actress
Diane Sawyer, December 22
news journalist

A neighborhood
afternoon picnic
often consisted of
homemade food,
horseshoes, croquet
and times of visiting
beneath spacious
shade trees.

Enjoying Family and Friends

Spending time with friends was one of the favorite pastimes for a nation looking to relax and enjoy life following high tensions from the war years.

One of the favorite activities occurred when groups of families brought food and joined together at someone's house for dinner and an afternoon of visiting and playing games such as croquet, horseshoes and baseball. The day would often conclude with making homemade ice cream.

In the evening, friends would often gather for a game of cards and late night snack, often consisting of homemade pastries. Neighborhood sings were also popular in 1945.

Friends would often get together to play various games while visiting for the evening. Those attending would often dress up in keeping with the more formal attire tradition of the time.

Campouts provided cheap weekend getaways. Fishing, cooking out and stargazing were often a part of such outings.

Sitting under a shade tree for a relaxing game of cards was always a good way to spend a summer afternoon.

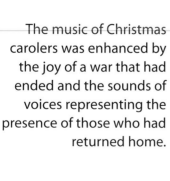

Home for Christmas

Christmas of 1945 was very emotional in many homes because it represented the first time that many entire families had been together in several years. Family members again occupied chairs that had been empty for Christmas dinner while they served in World War II.

In some cases, returning soldiers arrived just in time for Christmas celebrations. Some were forced to endure several connections in order to be at their home by Christmas morning.

Many of those who shared the joy of returning loved ones realized the importance of friendship and love versus gifts and material things. The warmth of a soldier's embrace was the greatest Christmas gift ever. How thankful everyone was to have loved ones home and alive.

The best Christmas gift possible was the embrace of a serviceman who was home with the family for Christmas.

The music of Christmas carolers was enhanced by the joy of a war that had ended and the sounds of voices representing the presence of those who had returned home.

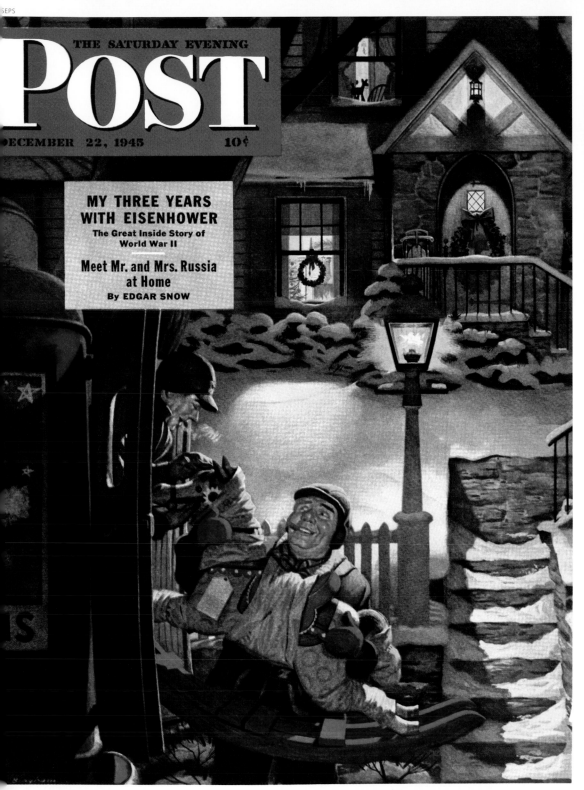

THE SATURDAY EVENING
POST

DECEMBER 22, 1945   10¢

MY THREE YEARS
WITH EISENHOWER
The Great Inside Story of
World War II

Meet Mr. and Mrs. Russia
at Home
By EDGAR SNOW

"Have you some little educational toy
that teaches advanced calculus?"

...eone will be very happy when seeing this hobby horse under the Christmas tree. One can only ...gine the excitement a lucky child will experience when it is discovered Christmas morning.

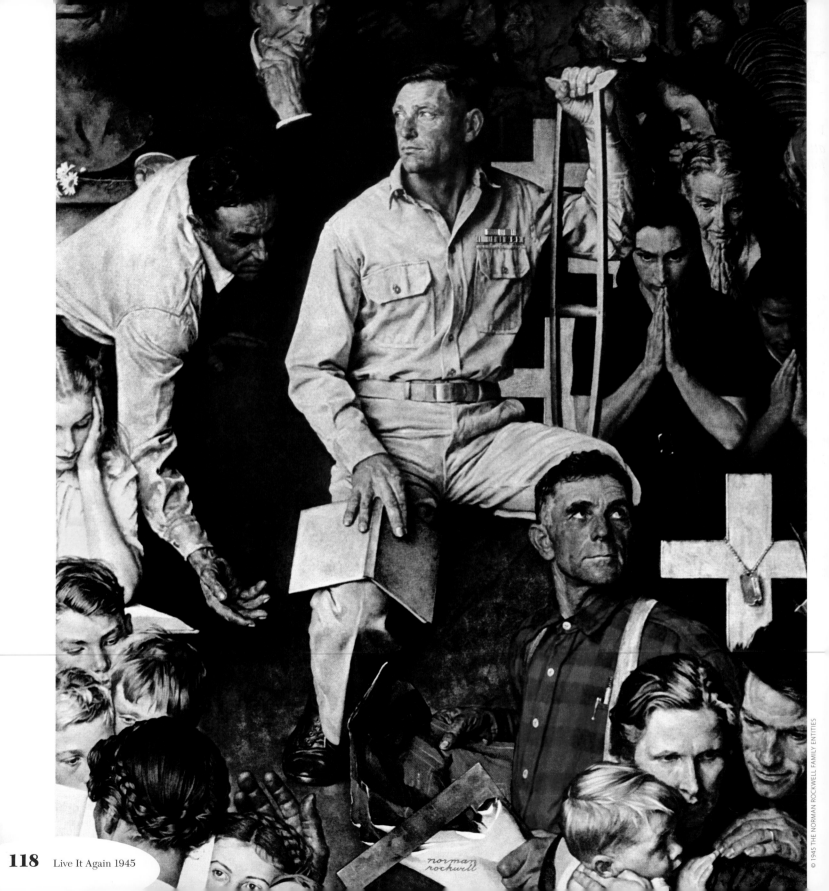

Yearning for a Better World

Editor's note: This Norman Rockwell painting and The Long Shadow of Lincoln *were featured together in the Feb. 10, 1945,* Post *magazine. In the heart-lifting symbolism of Rockwell's great painting there is thought for all of us. Here in the faces and attitudes of these people are determination and tolerance, all hoping for a better world. May we never forget what our soldiers fought and died for—our freedom.*

The Long Shadow of Lincoln
A *litany by Carl Sandburg*

We can succeed only by concert … The dogmas of the quiet past are inadequate to the stormy present. The occasion is piled high with difficulty, and we must rise with the occasion. As our case is new, so we must think anew and act anew. We must disenthrall ourselves … Dec. 1, 1862. The President Lincoln's Message to Congress.

Be sad, be cool, be kind.
Remembering those now dream-dust
Hallowed in the ruts and gullies,
Solemn bones under the smooth
    blue sea.
Faces war-blown in a falling rain.

Be a brother, if so can be,
To those beyond battle fatigue
Each in his own corner of earth
Or forty fathoms undersea
Beyond all boom of guns,
Beyond any bong of a great bell,
Each with a bosom and number,
Each with a pack of secrets,
Each with a personal dream
    and doorway,
And over them now the long
    endless winds
With the low healing song of time,
The hush and sleep murmur of time.
Make your wit a guard and cover.
Sing low, sing high, sing wide.
Let your laughter come free
Remembering looking toward peace:
"We must disenthrall ourselves."

Be a brother, if so can be,
To those thrown forward
For taking hard-won lines,
For holding hard-won points
And their reward so-so.
Little they care to talk about,
Their pay held in a mute calm,
High-spot memories going unspoken;
What they did being past words.
What they took being hard won.
Be sad, be kind, be cool.
Weep if you must.
And weep, open and shameless.
Before these altars.

There are wounds past words.
There are cripples less broken
Than many who walk whole.
There are dead youths
With wrists of silence
Who keep a vast music
Under their shut lips;
What they did being past words;
Their dreams, like their deaths
Beyond any smooth and easy telling;
Having given till no more to give.

There is dust alive
With dreams of the Republic,
With dreams of the family of man
Flung wide on a shrinking globe;
With old timetables,
Old maps, old guideposts
Torn into shreds,
Shot into tatters.

Burnt in a fire wind.
Lost in the shambles,
Faded in rubble and ashes.

There is dust alive.
Out of a granite tomb.
Out of a bronze sarcophagus,
Loose from the stone and copper
Steps a white-smoke ghost.
Lifting an authoritative hand
In the name of dreams worth dying for,
In the name of men whose dust breathes
Of those dreams so worth dying for;
What they did being past words.
Beyond all smooth and easy telling.

Be sad, be kind, be cool.
Remembering, under God, a dream-dust
Hallowed in the ruts and gullies.
Solemn bones under the smooth
    blue sea,
Faces war-blown in a falling rain.

Sing low, sing high, sing wide.
Make your wit a guard and cover.
Let your laughter come free
Like a help and a brace of comfort.

The earth laughs, the sun laughs
Over every wise harvest of man.
Over man looking toward peace
By the light of the hard old teaching:
"We must disenthrall ourselves."

More *The Saturday Evening Post Covers*

The Saturday Evening Post covers were works of art, many illustrated by famous artists of the time, including Norman Rockwell. Most of the 1945 covers have been incorporated within the previous pages of this book; the few that were not are presented on the following pages for your enjoyment.

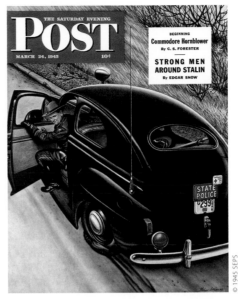

THE SATURDAY EVENING

POST

SEPTEMBER 22, 1945   10¢

THE SECRET HISTORY
OF A SURRENDER
By Forrest Davis

DEMAREE BESS
Reports on Sweden

THE SATURDAY EVENING

POST

OCTOBER 27, 1945   10¢

THE JAP SURRENDER
in full color

Demaree Bess reports
on the
BRITISH SOCIALISTS

THE SATURDAY EVENING

POST

NOVEMBER 3, 1945   10¢

CHICAGO
By
GEORGE SESSIONS PERRY

Beginning a new
ALBRAND SERIAL

norman rockwell

THE SATURDAY EVENING

POST

NOVEMBER 17, 1945   10¢

RUSSIA STILL
SUSPECTS US
By EDGAR SNOW

Corn Pays Off at Yale
By RED SMITH

Albert
Staehle

THE SATURDAY EVENING

POST

DECEMBER 1, 1945   10¢

A New Mystery by
ERLE STANLEY GARDNER

Blanchard: Greatest Fullback
of Them All?
By PETE MARTIN

THE SATURDAY EVENING

POST

DECEMBER 29, 1945   10¢

THE ALL-AMERICAN
TEAM

Europe's Most
Frightened Country
By ERNEST O. HAUSER

HAPPY NEW YEAR

norman rockwell

MORE FAMOUS BIRTHDAYS

January 3
Stephen Stills, rock singer and songwriter

January 4
Richard R. Schrock, chemist, Nobel Prize laureate

January 15
Joan Johnson, (The Dixie Cups)

January 17
William Hart, (The Delfonics)

January 20
Eric Stewart, singer and songwriter
   (The Mindbenders, 10cc)
Robert Olen Butler, writer

January 30
Michael Dorris, author

January 31
Joseph Kosuth, artist

February 6
Bob Marley, reggae superstar

February 9
Mia Farrow, actress

February 12
Maud Adams, actress

February 14
Vic Briggs, guitarist

February 20
Alan Hull, singer-songwriter (Lindisfarne)
Henry Polic II, comedian

February 25
Roy Saari, swimmer

February 27
Carl Anderson, singer and actor

February 28
Bubba Smith, football player and actor

March 4
Gary Williams, basketball coach

March 6
Hugh Grundy, (The Zombies)

March 7
John Heard, actor

March 8
Micky Dolenz, actor, director, and rock musician
   (The Monkees)

March 14
Walter Parazaider, (Chicago)
Jasper Carrott, comedian and singer

March 28
Charles Portz, (The Turtles)

March 29
Walt Frazier, basketball player

March 30
Eric Clapton, rock guitarist

March 31
Gabe Kaplan, actor, comedian, and professional
   poker player

April 9
Peter Gammons, baseball sportswriter
Steve Gadd, session drummer

April 13
Lowell George, rock musician
Bob Kalsu, football player

April 14
Ritchie Blackmore, English rock guitarist
   (Deep Purple)

April 25
Björn Ulvaeus, singer and songwriter (ABBA)
Stu Cook, (Creedence Clearwater Revival)

April 27
August Wilson, playwright

April 29
Tammi Terrell, soul singer

May 1
Rita Coolidge, pop singer

May 2
Goldy McJohn, Steppenwolf

May 5
Kurt Loder, film critic, author, and
   television personality

May 6
Bob Seger, rock singer

May 7
Christy Moore, folk musician

May 8
Keith Jarrett, pianist and composer

May 17
Tony Roche, tennis player

May 22
Victoria Wyndham, actress

May 23
Lauren Chapin, child actress and evangelist

June 1
Linda Scott, singer

June 4
Gordon Waller, singer (Peter and Gordon)

June 8
Steven Fromholz, singer-songwriter

June 11
Adrienne Barbeau, film and television actress

June 17
Frank Ashmore, actor

June 20
Anne Murray, singer

June 25
Carly Simon, singer and songwriter

July 1
Debbie Harry, singer (Blondie)

July 6
Burt Ward, actor

July 9
Dean Koontz, writer

July 11
Richard Wesley, playwright and screen writer

July 18
Danny McCulloch, (The Animals)

July 20
John Lodge, (The Moody Blues)
Kim Carnes, singer-songwriter

July 26
Betty Davis, singer

July 30
David Sanborn, saxophonist
Roger Dobkowitz, game show producer

August 1
Douglas D. Osheroff, physicist,
    Nobel Prize laureate

August 2
Joanna Cassidy, actress

August 4
Alan Mulally, businessman, CEO of the Ford
    Motor Company

August 7
Alan Page, football player

August 19
Ian Gillan, rock singer (Deep Purple)

August 22
Ron Dante, rock singer, songwriter, and record
    producer (The Archies)

August 24
Ronee Blakley, composer
Vince McMahon, professional wrestler, promoter,
    in-ring announcer, play-by-play commentator
    and film producer

August 31
Itzhak Perlman, violinist and conductor
Van Morrison, musician

September 4
Bill Kenwright, producer of West End musicals
Danny Gatton, guitarist

September 5
Al Stewart, singer-songwriter

September 8
Rogatien Vachon, former Canadian ice
    hockey player

September 9
Dee Dee Sharp, R&B singer

September 15
Jessye Norman, soprano

September 19
David Bromberg, guitarist
Randolph Mantooth, actor and motivational
    speaker

September 21
Kay Ryan, poet

September 23
Paul Peterson, former child actor and advocate
    of other former child actors

September 24
John Rutter, composer

September 25
Dee Dee Warwick, singer

October 3
Kay Baxter, bodybuilder

October 4
Clifton Davis, actor

October 12
Dusty Rhodes, professional wrestler

October 13
Susan Stafford, television presenter

October 15
Jim Palmer, baseball player

October 19
Jeannie C. Riley, country singer

October 25
David Schramm, astrophysicist

October 28
Wayne Fontana, singer

October 29
Melba Moore, singer and actress

October 31
Brian Doyle, actor

November 12
Michael Bishop, author
Tracy Kidder, journalist and author
Neil Young, Canadian musician

November 15
Anni-Frid Lyngstad, singer (ABBA)

November 20
Dan McBride, (Sha Na Na)

November 23
Jerry Harris, sculptor

November 24
Lee Michaels, keyboardist and singer

November 26
Daniel Davis, actor

December 4
Eileen O'Brien, British actress

December 13
Kathy Garver, actress

December 14
Stanley Crouch, music critic

December 16
Patti Deutsch, voice actress

December 17
Ernie Hudson, actor
Chris Matthews, news author

December 19
Elaine Joyce, actress and game show panelist

December 25
Gary Sandy, actor

December 26
John Walsh, media personality

December 30
Davy Jones, actor
    and singer (The Monkees)

Facts and Figures of 1945

President of the U.S.
Franklin D. Roosevelt until his death April 12, 1945
Vice President of the U.S.
Harry S. Truman until April 12, 1945
President of the U.S.
Harry S. Truman sworn in April 12, 1945
Vice President of the U.S.
None appointed

Population of the U.S.
139,928,165

Births
2,858,000

US ARMY, COURTESY OF HARRY S. TRUMAN LIBRARY

College Graduates
Males: 58,664
Females: 77,510

Average Salary for full-time employee: $2,259.00
Minimum Wage (per hour): $0.40

Average cost for:

Bread (lb.)	$0.09
Bacon (lb.)	$0.41
Butter (lb.)	$0.51
Eggs (doz.)	$0.58
Milk (1/2 gal.)	$0.31
Potatoes (10 lbs.)	$0.49
Coffee (lb.)	$0.31
Sugar (5 lb.)	$0.33
Gasoline (gal.)	$0.15
Movie Ticket	$0.35
Postage Stamp	$0.03
Car	$1,020.00
Single-Family home	$4,600.00

REPRINTED WITH PERMISSION FROM FORD MOTOR COMPANY

Notable Inventions and Firsts

January 15: *Art Linkletter's House Party* debuts on CBS radio.

April 19: Rodgers & Hammerstein musical *Carousel* opens on Broadway.

August 16: President Truman lifts the wartime wage freeze but said wages could be increased only if the increases did not force price increases. He ordered full resumption of consumer-goods production August 18 with a return to free markets and collective bargaining between labor and management.

August 22: Vietnam conflict begins as Ho Chi Minh leads a successful coup.

September 8: American troops occupy southern Korea, while the Soviet Union occupies the north, with dividing line being the 38th parallel of latitude. This arrangement proves to be the indirect beginning of a divided Korea.

September: Henry Ford steps down from the presidency of Ford Motor Company at age 82 as production of civilian passenger car resumes.

December: The U.S. War Production Board lifts its wartime ban on the manufacture of radio and television equipment for consumer use.

Son of Lassie, the second Lassie film, becomes the first movie ever to be filmed using the Technicolor Monobook method, where a single magazine of film was used to record all of the primary colors.

The American Cancer Society is created by a renaming of the American Society for the Control of Cancer founded in 1913.

Fluoridation of a water supply to prevent dental decay is introduced in Grand Rapids, Mich.

Sports Winners

NCAA Men's Basketball: Oklahoma A&M defeats New York University

NFL: Cleveland Rams defeat Washington Redskins

World Series: Detroit Tigers defeat Chicago Cubs

Stanley Cup: Toronto Maple Leafs defeat Detroit Red Wings

The Masters: Not played due to World War II

PGA Championship: Byron Nelson

Live It Again 1945

PROJECT EDITOR	Barb Sprunger
ART DIRECTOR	Brad Snow
COPYWRITERS	Becky Sarasin, Jim Langham
COPY SUPERVISOR	Deborah Morgan
PRODUCTION ARTIST SUPERVISOR	Erin Augsburger
PRODUCTION ARTIST	Erin Augsburger
COPY EDITOR	Amanda Scheerer
PHOTOGRAPHY SUPERVISOR	Tammy Christian
NOSTALGIA EDITOR	Ken Tate
EDITORIAL DIRECTOR	Jeanne Stauffer
PUBLISHING SERVICES DIRECTOR	Brenda Gallmeyer

Printed in China
First Printing: 2011
Library of Congress Control Number: 2010904351
ISBN: 978-1-59217-308-2

Customer Service
LiveItAgain.com
(800) 829-5865

1 2 3 4 5 6 7 8 9